MW01626814

Under the Lighthouse

Memories of Barnegat City

Mary Karch

DOWN THE SHORE
PUBLISHING
Harvey Cedars, New Jersey

Mr. and Mrs. Skawder, friends of John Engelsen (facing page), on the dunes in Barnegat City, 1936.

Down The Shore Publishing Corp., Box 3100, Harvey Cedars, NJ 08008
www.down-the-shore.com
The words "Down The Shore" and the Down The Shore Publishing logos are registered U.S. Trademarks.

Book design by Leslee Ganss

Manufactured in China
10 9 8 7 6 5 4 3 2 1
First printing, 2004.

Library of Congress Cataloging-in-Publication Data

Karch, Mary.
Under the lighthouse : memories of Barnegat City / Mary Karch
p. cm
ISBN 1-59322-012-X
1. Barnegat Light (N.J.)--History--Pictorial works. 2. Barnegat Light (N.J.)--History. I. Title.

F144.B23K37 2004
974.9'48--dc22

2004052710

To my parents, Mr. and Mrs. Darrell Montgomery,
my sister Theresa, and brothers Bill and Tom.
And to the families I grew to love in Barnegat Light,
this book is for you.

Old wooden causeway bridge, Manahawkin

Brownsville

JAMES M. MILLER, Auctioneer

VALUABLE IMPROVED & UNIMPROVED PROPERTY At Barnegat Inlet,

Now owned by JNO. A. BROWN, Esq., consisting of DWELLING HOUSE, BOWLING ALLEY, AND OUT-BUILDINGS, And 30 Acres of Land.

JAMES M. MILLER will sell at Auction,

On FRIDAY, AUGUST 20th, 1869,

At the Hotel of COWDRICK & COOK, TOMS RIVER, at 2 o'clock, P. M.,

The above named Valuable Property, comprising over 30 acres, situate on Barnegat Inlet, adjoining the Light House. The advantages of the Inlet property excel any other property of the kind on the coast of New-Jersey. It has the finest bathing, the best hook and line fishing, the finest Bay for sailing, plenty of shade trees, with bold water right up to the property. It offers one of the best chances for any one with capital to run a small steamer from the Inlet to Toms River through the Boarding season, and can be made second to no place on the coast of New Jersey, south of Long Branch. Cars leave Philadelphia, by the 6 o'clock Camden and Amboy train by way of Freehold, and New York by 9 o'clock boat of R. & D. B. R. R., and be at the Inlet at 2 o'clock, P. M. Leave the Inlet at 9 A. M., and connect with the mid-day train for New York or Philadelphia.

TERMS.—10 per cent. on day of sale; balance in 60 days, when Deed will be given.

Maps at the Office of the Auctioneer, 28 Pine Street, New York City; G. Castor Smith, Engineer 4th Light House dist., Philadelphia; George M. Joy, New Jersey Courier, Toms River, or

JOHN A. BROWN, Barnegat.

Auction announcement for the property of Captain John Brown, who bought up large tracts of land, and the Herring House, in 1855. Everything outside the government-owned lighthouse area was known as Brownsville. Brown sold everything after his son drowned at sea. At the bottom of the poster is this description of the area: "The advantages of the Inlet property excel any other property of the kind on the coast of New Jersey. It has the finest bathing, the best hook and line fishing, the finest Bay for sailing, plenty of shade trees, with bold water right up to the property. If offers one of the best chances for any one with capital to run a small steamer from the Inlet to Toms River through the Boarding season, and can be made second to no place on the coast of New Jersey, south of Long Branch."

Introduction

When my family came to Barnegat City it was not clear what kind of a life lay ahead of us. Like that journey, it was not always clear what form this book would take. Why did I gather these old pictures, draw upon the memories of previous residents of Barnegat Light — this small town, one rich in history, full of people dedicated to the sea. What did I want to learn about this fishing village, peopled by immigrants from Norway, who were able to haul a living from the sea? Did I want to retrace my childhood, relive a time when I went to school in a one-room schoolhouse, kept warm by a pot-bellied stove in the winter? Perhaps my story is not so different from others who have settled in Barnegat Light in its early days. And perhaps like theirs, my story starts with my father. He was the reason why we came to this island, but perhaps not the reason we stayed.

I know now that there was something extraordinary here. A town sparsely populated, but full of strong, independent people. Barnegat City— with its lighthouse, its shifting shores, its promises of hot summers, plentiful fish for all those willing to work —had more to offer than just the familiar lighthouse. We have used that lighthouse to guide our ships, to watch for enemy ships during the war. We have known it as a constant in our lives, something that, if protected, will not give in to weather and time. Even as other landmarks have aged, or, like the lighthouse keeper's house, abandoned and torn down.

This book is a photographic reminder of the roles the lighthouse, the sea, the people have played in the making of a community — so changed by industry, by residents, by the march of time. The same bridge that delivered my family would deliver more families. And new bridges, like the new causeway built in 1958, would as well. Seekers of sun, seekers of new kind of life would move here and permanently change what I had found when my family came to Barnegat Light.

But the memories are worth preserving, memories of change, in contrast with the steady lighthouse, the rise and decline of the fishing industry — of the people, past and present, who keep the "light" of the town alive.

East Bay Avenue, Manahawkin. This was the road to the bridge and Long Beach Island, circa 1900.

1920: The orignal causeway was built in 1914 and remained in use until the new causeway was built in 1958. Note the train trestle on the right, which was built in 1886.

In 1937, Darrell and Betty Montgomery took their two children and moved from Philadelphia, Pa. to the Jersey Shore. Darrell, along with his brother Joel, had found work in a small town on the north end of Long Beach Island, a place called Barnegat City.

There was a lot of work for men at the fisheries in this small town. Darrell and his brother both knew a lot about boats from working the shipyards in Philadelphia. Though my brother Billy and I were little, I can remember riding for a very long time, and all we could see were pines for miles. There was hardly a house around. Mom was getting a little nervous — she had no idea where she was going. Being a city gal, this was all new to her.

We made it through the pines and came to a town called Manahawkin, and soon we came to a thicket of trees. Suddenly the sky opened up to a great marsh, with shanties along the shore, creeks going in all directions, wild flowers growing out of the reeds on the banks. And finally up ahead a bit was the bridge. Billy and I were jumping from one side of the car to the other, trying to see the water. Mom wanted to know where we were going — Dad never told her she was going to be living on an island, surrounded by water, and this really got her upset since she couldn't swim.

Over the bridge we went. To the right was another narrow bridge and Dad said it was used back in the old days for the train to run across. Well, mom said, this sure does look like the "old days".

One more bridge to go, said Dad. As we approached the gates came down and bells began to ring — the bridge was opening; and we waited while a small boat passed under it. Then over we went, and down on to a small two-lane road, past a clam house and a few small houses, until we came to a circle and we had to stop.

Up ahead you could see the beach with boats and nets hanging from poles. In the middle was a fishery and a diner, a small store called Junky Johns, and a bath house on the corner.

We made a left turn and headed north. We passed a hotel, a church, a few houses, and then nothing but brush. There were wild roses growing all over along the roadside, and vines with red and black berries. We could see the dunes every now and then, and at times the bay was real close to the road. All of a sudden we saw a big hotel, standing tall, and it looked like it was in the bay.

The next little town had a post office and a general store. Dad called the place Harvey Cedars. He stopped at the general store and asked if they knew where Joel Montgomery was living, and got directions. When Dad and Uncle Joel were at the shore earlier that year, Dad rented a small cottage for us; Joel had already moved here with his family. When we got to Uncle Joel's, only 2 blocks away, he took dad over to our new house. It was just a two-story cottage, a summer rental, but we were staying year round. Mom was not thrilled at what she saw, and wanted to know what the small house out back was used

Children in the brush by the railroad station, Barnegat City, 1941. Left to right: Mary Reynolds, Jack Roberts, Mary Montgomery, William Montgomery. When this photograph was taken the Montgomerys were living at the station.

for. Dad said it was the outhouse. Mom gave him a look, she didn't have to say anything, he knew she didn't like it.

Mom fixed the house up real nice for us, but when winter started rolling in it sure did get cold. The floor in the kitchen would blow up and down with the wind, and the lights would go off and on. Mom would bundle us up, and let us go out to play. One day we got a little to far from the house; we didn't know we could get into any trouble, but lo and behold, I fell into this swampy ditch. Billy tried to pull me out and couldn't. He ran back to the house and got mom, who came a running. By now I was sucked down a bit further in the mud, so she pulled and pulled until I finally broke free, but my shoes were pulled right off my feet.

The winters were so cold and the wind was blowing all the time. And there were ice storms, where the power lines would come down and then we would have no electricity. We had a kerosene stove to heat the house, and hung blankets in the doorway to keep the cold out, and keep the heat in one room.

After we spent the winter in this cold house, mom said she was going back to the city if we didn't move to a warmer house before next winter. So Dad started looking for a new place for us to live. He was working for Mr. Sunquist at the time, building boats. Mr. Sunquist was the only boat builder in Barnegat City, and we loved to go to the big old wooden shed where the boats were being built; it always smelled like cedar chips. There were so many things to see there — the big grinding wheel, and big saws. Mr. Sunquist told Dad that the old railroad station was for rent; a Mrs. Penn had bought it and made two apartments out of it. So Uncle Joel and Aunt Cass took the bottom floor and we took the second floor. The house sat right in the middle of the marsh,

Mary Montgomery on the beach at East 5th Street, Barnegat City, in 1938 with her dog Abe. The structure on the far left is a wooden tower that the Coast Guard used as a lookout.

between what is now 11th and 12th Streets on the bay side. The railroad station was big but it had no running water; we had to go to the pump house for water every day, and we still had an outside privy.

At that time the town consisted of a few big houses on 12th Street, a few more in the center of town, a post office and two bars. There was a little schoolhouse and a Coast Guard Station; the rest was all brush and woods. The roads were either sand or gravel, and most were just broken clam shells.

Now this was not quite the place where mom wanted to live, but it had to do for now. We just loved it here, Billy and I. We were always barefoot, and the place was full of pricker-burrs

— we were stepping on them all the time. For us, it was a place full of adventure. I liked the wild side of things and the feel of the earth under my bare feet. Billy and I could walk to the bay and watch the small fish swim around, and the fiddler crabs run for their holes as soon as we would come close. In the summer we would find turtle eggs, buried in the sand, and the cat birds with their nests so low in the trees, we could count the eggs. We never knew where the red-winged black birds built their nests, but there were plenty of them. Barn sparrows would build nests all around the railroad station, high up in the beams. Skate eggs were all over the beach, and when you shook one it sounded just like a rattle. Sometimes starfish washed up on the beach by the thousands, and clams too. It was like we were meant be in this place, so quiet yet so full of life. Finally, we were home.

At the Independent Dock, West 18th Street: Mary Roberts (Mary's grandmother), Mary Montgomery, Helen Morris (aunt), and Bill Montgomery.

PLAN OF

BARNEGAT CITY,

SITUATED AT BARNEGAT INLET,
N.J.
LONG BEACH.

SCALE

THE REGULAR SIZE OF LOTS is 50 feet front by 125 feet deep

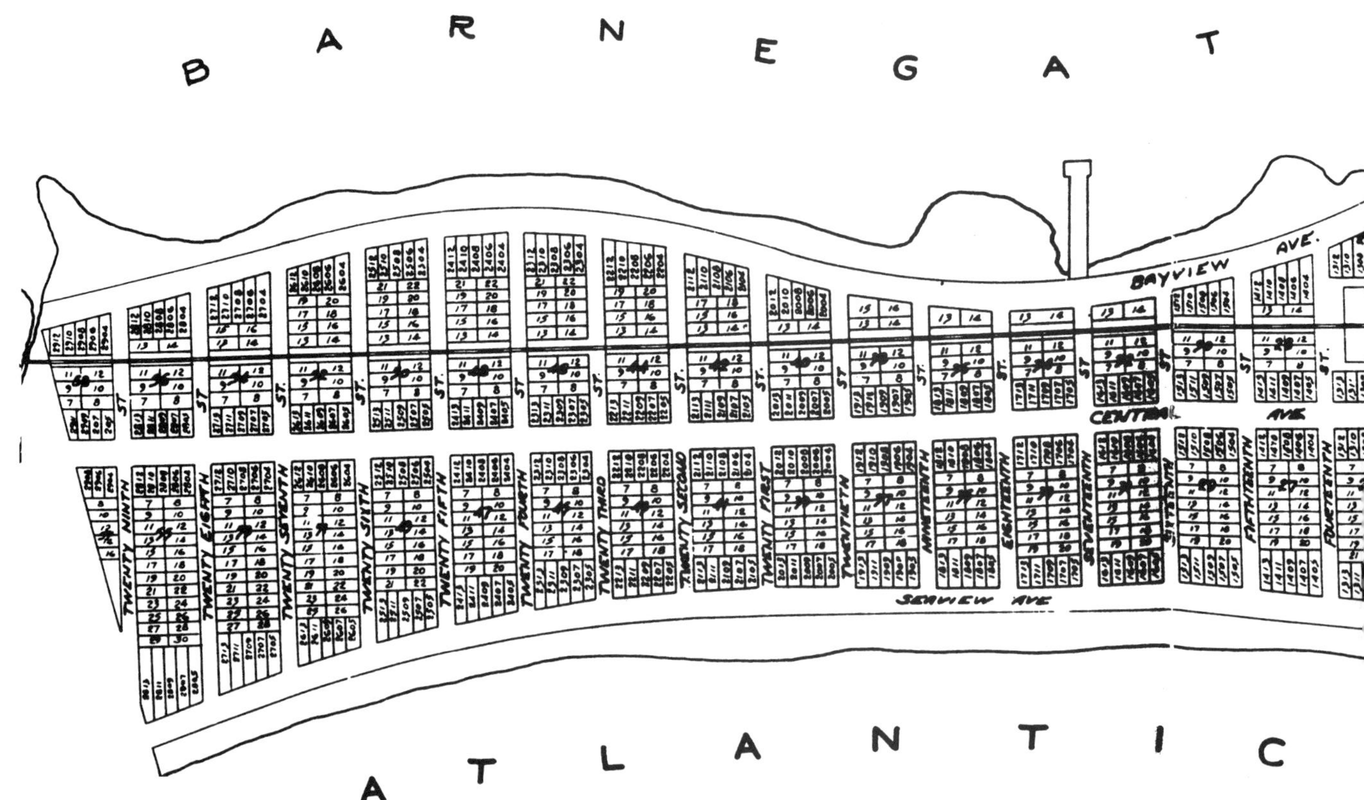

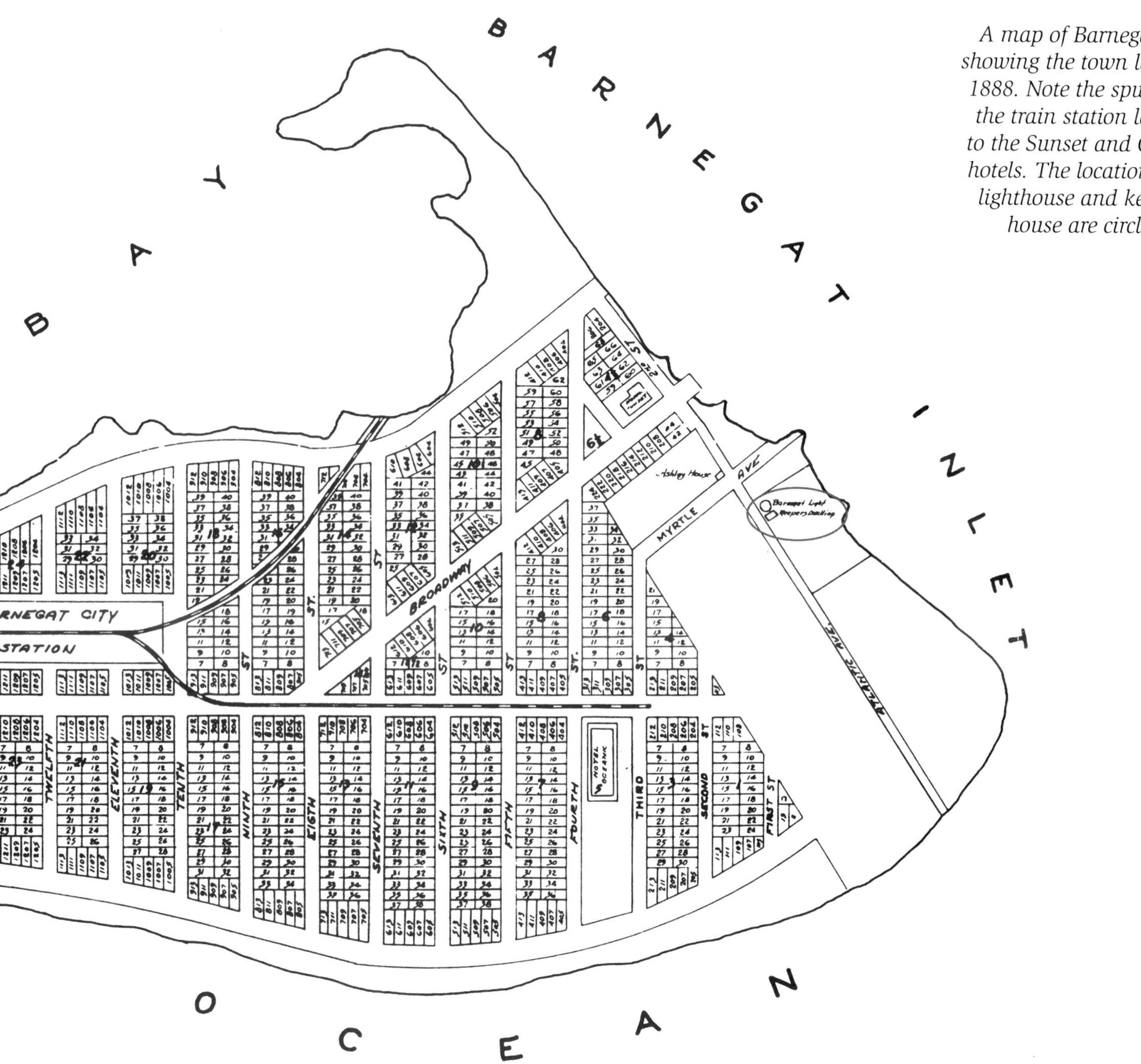

A map of Barnegat City showing the town layout in 1888. Note the spurs from the train station leading to the Sunset and Oceanic hotels. The location of the lighthouse and keeper's house are circled.

Barnegat City Timeline

1609 Henry Hudson, while surveying the coast in the *Half Moon*, described Barnegat Bay and Barnegat Inlet in his ship's log: "We came to a great lake of water, as we could judge it to be ...The mouth of the lake hath many shoals, and the sea breaketh on them as it is cast out of the mouth of it."

1614 Captain Cornelius Jacobsen Mey named what Hudson had described as *Barende-gat*, which translates as "Inlet of Breakers."

1678 Licence granted for whaling between Barnegat Inlet and Eastern Provinces

1740s Sawmills in Barnegat, Stafford, and Toms River shipped lumber through Barnegat Inlet to markets in New York.

1750 Cranberry Inlet opened in the barrier beach across from Toms River. Ships could take the more direct route to go north rather than go the circuitous route through Barnegat Inlet.

1782 October 26, Barnegat Light Massacre —A Belgian cutter going south ran ashore near the inlet. Captain Andrew Steelman noticed the ship and had local men unload it. While they were resting on the beach they were attacked by Captain John Bacon and his loyalist friends; almost all of Steelman's men were murdered.

1795 Caleb Parker is the first settler at Barnegat Inlet.

1800s The area surrounding Barnegat Inlet was used for camping, mostly by vacationing farmers.

1814 Early settlers Bart Slaight and his wife Ruth buy lowlands and beaches along the inlet and build a small house.

1825 Slaight builds large home to accommodate boarders; later sells it to Jacob Herring, who called it the Herring House and catered to gunners from New York and Philadelphia.

1834 Slaight sells 5 acres to the U.S. Government, with the stipulation that no stores or taverns be built, nor could cattle roam the grounds.

1835 First Barnegat Lighthouse tower built. It was a forty-foot tall white-washed brick structure, designed by Winslow Lewis. With the close of Cranberry Inlet, merchant ships once again used Barnegat Inlet for shipping.

A view of Barnegat City from the top of the lighthouse, circa 1910, looking southeast, at the intersection of Central Avenue and 4th Street. The train, "Tar Pot," is making her turn around the switch track and turntable. The Oceanic Hotel dominates the landscape. The building beyond the hotel is the enlarged lifesaving ltation.

1854 Fourth-order Fresnel lens installed in light station to improve the quality of light, but the decaying building was too short to project light a good distance.

1855 Captain John Brown buys Herring House, renaming it Ashley House, as well as a large portion of the area. Except for the government-owned lighthouse, the area becomes known as Brownsville.
Lieutenant George G. Meade begins designing a new lighthouse.
House of Refuge built at Barnegat Inlet; it was an unmanned shelter for shipwreck victims.

1856 The first lighthouse tower falls into the sea; Construction begins on the new lighthouse.

1859 Construction completed on new tower, with a first-order Fresnel lens. Lighthouse is commissioned in January.

1869 John Brown's 30-acres of land is put up for auction.

c.1872 U.S. Lifesaving Service builds Station #17 at Barnegat, as well as others along the Jersey Shore. It was redesigned/rebuilt two more times in the 1880s.

1874 John Brown sells Ashley House to Charles Martin.

1881 Benjamin Franklin Archer forms Barnegat City Improvement Company. Barnegat City becomes the unofficial name of the town. The *Hesse*, a steamer working with the Pennsylvania Railroad, picks up passengers from New York and Trenton and takes them to the landing pier at Barnegat Inlet. The *Connetquot* soon replaces her.
Construction begins on the Oceanic Hotel.

1882 Oceanic Hotel opens.
John Warner Kinsey buys the Ashley House, renaming it the Kinsey Hotel. Later Kinsey would move to Harvey Cedars, abandoning the hotel.

1883 Construction begins on the Sans Souci, a hotel, hoping to attract winter sportsmen.

1884 Another small hotel, The Social, opens to boarders.
The Barnegat and Long Beach Improvement Co. purchase land to be used for right-of-way, station and other railroad uses.

1886 Manahawkin and Long Beach Railroad completed. First train reached Barnegat City on June 28.

1889 The triple-keeper's house is built by the Federal Lighthouse Bureau to house the three keepers and their families.

1899 Benjamin Archer sells the Sans Souci, and the name is changed to the Sunset Hotel, but business declines after the railroad is built. Lifesaving Service acts as look out for enemy ships during the Spanish-American War. Signal House built for signaling ships offshore. War ends shortly after Signal House is built.

1903 New school is built in town.

1904 Barnegat City secedes from Long Beach (township) and becomes an official town.

1914 Oceanic closes. John Barber buys the Sunset Hotel. Automobile bridge to the island opens.

1915 U.S. Lifesaving Service merges with Revenue Cutter Service to become the U.S. Coast Guard.

First Presbyterian Church (now St. Peters), Central Avenue and West 7th Street This was the first church in Barnegat City, built by Benjamin Archer in 1889 for guests of the Oceanic Hotel (in the distance on the right). Town meetings were also held here in its early days. The church was closed in the winter.

1919-20 Winter storms threaten Barnegat City with flooding and erosion.

1920 Captain Dick Myers opens pound fishery. Keepers' house sold by Federal Lighthouse Bureau when erosion threatens the structure.

1921 Myers buys 33 acres, from West 7th Street to the bay.

1926 Railroad ends operations to Barnegat City.

1927 Scandinavian fishermen in Barnegat City begin to form the Independent Fishery.

1932 Sunset Hotel burns to the ground

1933 Coastal storm washes over the town from theinlet to the bay. Airship *Akron* crashes in sea near Barnegat Inlet.

1935 Railroad bridge washes out, rail service ends on Long Beach Island.

1942 World War II. Beaches patrolled by Coast Guard.

1944 Major Hurricane hits Long Beach Island and the Jersey Shore.

1945 World War II ends.

1948 Barnegat City changes name to Barnegat Light.

1950 Dragger fishing ends in Barnegat Light. Tile fishing begins.
Gill-netting makes a comeback from a decline in the 1920s.

1951 One-room school house closes.

1958 New causeway bridge opens.

Haddock House, Signal House, one-room schoolhouse, Coast Guard station, and three of the original houses from 1883 are located in this 1955 aerial photograph looking down at 7th Street, facing north to Island Beach.

Barnegat City

Looking west from the ocean around 1886. The Oceanic is on the right, and was later moved back because of beach erosion. The homes are the first of the 26 built by Archer and his Barnegat City Improvement Company.

1886-1926: Barnegat City railroad station. This two-story building had hand pumps for water on the first floor and an outhouse in back. Benjamin Archer's home is in the distance just to the right of the station.

The Manahawkin and Long Beach Railroad's "Old Yellow Jacket" in front of the Oceanic Hotel. From left to right: Alfred Brown, Morton Crane, Alex Inman, Clarence Bennett. The train ran between Manahawkin and Barnegat City Monday, Wednesday and Friday.

The Social, around 1900 (right), and just after it was built (below) in 1884. The Social was owned and operated by the Kroeger family, who rented rooms to hunters and served three meals a day. The third hotel in Barnegat City, it was smaller than the others but did very well in the fall hunting season, attracting sportsmen from Philadelphia and New York. Mrs. Kroeger's granddaughter, Juanita Kelly, remembers roller skating all around the front porch.

The Oceanic Hotel

Construction of the Oceanic Hotel began in 1881 on the north side of East 4th Street. Benjamin Franklin Archer, of the Barnegat City Improvement Company, wanted to model his hotel after the popular resorts on the south end of the island.

Mrs. Zeber remembers the Oceanic Hotel.

"There were four floors. Each floor had red carpeting throughout the hallway. The first floor had the dining room on the right side and the office was on the left. People would come into the office to make arrangements for next summer, to pay their bill. The next floor was filled with bedrooms and the ballroom, with its parquet floor, and a piano to the side, perhaps on a small stage. When one tired of dancing there were other side rooms where guests could play cards or read, knit and talk. The third floor and the fourth floor were all bedrooms, a few bathrooms to be shared by guests."

Typical of the time, dunes were leveled when a hotel was built, perhaps to provide an easy walk from the steps of the hotel, a clear view. To a modern visitor the Oceanic would have looked without protection, without battlements against a floodtide, a stern northeaster, against remarkable erosion. In 1884, the hotel was moved from the north side of 4th Street several hundred feet back from the ocean, a defensive move against nature, but visitors were not flocking to the Oceanic Hotel as expected. In 1886 the Manahawkin and Long Beach Railroad train made its first appearance at the hotel. Benjamin Archer was one of the catalysts to bring the railroad to town, to help bring more business to the town.

In 1910 typhoid fever struck, killing one hotel guest. The Oceanic was closed for two seasons, reopened, and then closed for good in 1914.

The Oceanic had long been empty. When he was about 15, around 1919, Morris Archer's family stayed during a northeaster. The storm came up and stayed for two days. The second night of the storm, Mrs. Archer wanted to see what the ocean looked like, perhaps to see if the storm had eroded the beach and if the tide would flood their home if they stayed. Mrs. Archer and Morris walked up Central Avenue to the Oceanic. The area around the Oceanic was nothing but flat beach and the hotel. Just the afternoon before the storm he had fished for flounders off the beach for dinner. He was surprised when the lighthouse beam came round, illuminating what had been in shadow — what he expected to be sand and dune grass was now water and wreckage. The tide had run very strong and had washed away most of the beach up to the steps of the Oceanic in twenty-four hours.

The Oceanic wasn't taken in any one storm, but slowly, as the ocean ate away at it, the tides came in to take out more wood, more foundation, until finally nothing was left of the rear portion of the building.

Annex in the rear of the Oceanic Hotel after a two-day ice storm in 1920.

The Sunset Hotel

The Sunset Hotel, 1929.

The second hotel built by Archer, the Sunset Hotel, began its career as the Sans Souci. Benjamin Franklin Archer and the Barnegat City Improvement Company built the Sans Souci in 1883. San Souci was a fitting name for a place billed as "Fisherman's Paradise" and "Sportsman's Haven," but the name would have fit better had people filled the hotel near to its capacity of 150 guests. The hotel had its own pier and easy access to the inlet and the bay. In 1887, because of decreasing business, Archer sold the hotel for $20,000 to a syndicate from Pennsylvania. The name of the hotel was changed to the Sunset, but business began to decline even more. When the Oceanic (also owned by Archer) closed, supposedly because of cases of typhoid fever in 1910, the Sunset closed as well. The

The Sunset Hotel, 1920, in a view from the top of the lighthouse. You can see the long pier where guest arrived and departed by boat on the right. Below, Lewis Jones of Barnegat, driver for Captain Myers, helps Dick Myers Jr. off the bus which took guests from the steamer pier to the Oceanic. Freda (Benestad) Fackler is behind them on the bus.

Sunset reopened in 1914 under the ownership of John Barber, who sold it in 1924 to Captain A. R. (Dick) Myers. Myers remodeled the hotel, updating the electrical wires, plumbing, the kitchen, and all of the bedrooms. The hotel flooded in May of 1932, and burned down on June 26, 1932. The brick and wire remains of the structure were washed into the bay in succeeding storms and tides.

1929: Lewis Jones, at the steamer pier north of the Sunset Hotel, waits for the Connetquot *to take him across the bay to Barnegat on the mainland.*

The Connetquot, *circa 1888, a paddle-wheeled, steam-driven yacht, traveled across the bay from Barnegat to Barnegat City, bringing guests to the Sunset and Oceanic Hotels. She could carry about 30 passengers and had quarters for all aboard. On the far right is the Sunset Hotel, to the left of that is Andy Bjornberg Sr.'s home. Behind the hotel is a rare glimpse of a white-washed Barnegat Lighthouse, in the midst of being repainted.*

The Sunset Girls

Not just girls: (from left to right) Alice Francis, Loran Midgett, Frances Engelsen, Nores Wagner, Halton Midgett, Mrs. Peterson (the cook), 1926.

Memories of Ann (Engelsen) Suralik:

"Mom (Frances Engelsen) would tell me how she and her girlfriends would all come to the shore during the summer, from Pennsylvania State College, and work as waitresses. In 1924 they worked and stayed at the Sunset Hotel. That is how they got the name the "Sunset Girls". They came year after year, making friends with the local fishermen. Everyone enjoyed a day off from work and a ride out to sea with a captain of a fishing vessel."

The "Sunset Girls" in 1930, enjoying a day off. Left to right: Grace DeLoach, Betty Hartman, Bertha Johnston, Francis Englesen.

The General Store

Barnegat City's general store and post office was built around 1875.
Above: Mrs. Buttersworth, circa 1900

Lucrecia Buttersworth first ran the post office and store on the north side of 4th Street and Central Avenue. It was said she didn't like to sell her goods because it took too long to get new supplies in, and one could only purchase medicine in an emergency — if she judged it as such. In 1919 the business was sold to the Applegates. Mr. Applegate was the lighthouse keeper and a net fisherman. On a fishing trip his button got caught in the net and he was pulled overboard and drowned. Mrs. Applegate ran the store and the post

Barnegat Light post office, as it appeared in 1950, on East 18th Street.

office until 1950, when the post office relocated to 18th Street.

Before it was a post office, the 18th Street building was a general store and gas station, first owned by Jens Jensen in 1920, who gave it to John Englesen in 1940 as a trade for John's house on 19th Street. It served as Barnegat Light's post office until the current facility on West 10th Street opened. Today Barnegat Light has the distinction of having the only deviating ZIP code on Long Beach Island (08006).

A frequent canine customer, Sinbad, waits for the bar to open

Kubel's Bar

Located on West 7th Street, Kubel's was built in 1920 and first owned by Paul Ketzel, and known as Ketzel's Bar. Rooms were let out to fishermen, and it was the local spot for a night out. The second owner, "Ma" Kubel, served meals in the small dining room addition by the bar, and hosted local parties featuring Norwegian dancing. Today, Kubel's is still a familiar landmark in Barnegat Light.

Sinbad the Sailor

Sinbad in front of the Barnegat Coast Guard Station on East 7th Street with some of his cronies.

Sinbad, the Coast Guard dog, would often stop by Kubel's for a glass of beer. Ma Kubel would set a glass of beer and a saucer on the bar for the customers to pour for the dog, who arrived wearing a little coat bearing his rank (he was a Navy hero), and a small barrel around his neck which contained his beer money — although he was almost always treated by a Coast Guardsman or another customer at the bar. The mixed-breed died in 1951, and is buried under the flagpole at the Coast Guard station.

Located on West 8th Street, in 1919 this building was owned by Magna Hansen and called the Barnegat City Tea Shop and served sweets, coffee, and of course, tea. Later it was sold to Ingman Benestad and renamed the Barnegat City Inn (left), and was a favorite family restaurant. In the 1940s-50s, Josie Rider ran it as a boarding house and restaurant. Its most well-known incarnation was as Wida's Restaurant. It became a popular landmark for vacationers and locals alike, as well as providing summer jobs to many children.

The Barnegat City Inn

"Full course dinner was 50 cents and homemade. Mom was the cook, and I would help out waiting on tables. I remember one night a couple came in. I waited on them, I was a pretty good waitress but they had me running back and forth, getting this and that. When it was time for them to leave he gave me the money for their dinners and said there would be something for me. I took the money to mother and went back to clean up the table, there was a dime left. I picked up the dime and saw them just about to leave, and my mother saw what I was about to do — I ran over to him and said. 'Here, you need this more than I do.' Mother was angry with me and said 'Why did you do that?!' I just said 'At least they could have left me a quarter!'"

—Freda (Benestad) Fackler

The One-Room Schoolhouse

1948: Eddie Eliason, Harry Hansen, Brian Engelsen, first-graders who would eventually be part of the last class of the one-room schoolhouse.

Gloria Hansen Braun remembers the one-room schoolhouse:

She recalls that she hit Jerome Walnut with a history book. "I was trying to hit Dick Myers," who eventually came to own the local pound fishery.

"We walked to school every day."

Once she arrived at school, Gloria often found herself standing behind the big black stove because she had misbehaved.

"My brother, David Hansen, he was always hunting ducks. He would get off the school bus a

Above: During one of the last years of the schoolhouse, the girls dressed up in ethnic costumes, celebrating their Scandinavian heritage. Right: The school as it appeared in 1903.

few blocks away from home so Mom wouldn't know. He hid his gun the night before in the bushes."

The first and only Girl Scout troop of Barnegat Light — "Lone Troop 1," Memorial Day, 1935. From left; Florence Applegate, Helen Johnson, Ingeborg Hansen, Juanita Kelly, Martha Hoff, Kare Hansen and Freda Benestad

"Lone Troop 1"

It was called the Lone Troop 1, our Scout leader was from Beach Haven and she was affiliated with the Episcopal Church. What a good person she was — wanted to help the children of Barnegat City."

— Freda (Benestad) Fackler

The children of Barnegat Light on D-Day; the fire truck took them for a ride to 18th Street, then they walked to the fire hall for a party, waving their flags.

"Many of the women worked the Civil Defense watching for planes from the fire hall. Gudney Svelling was in charge, and David Hansen Sr. was the air raid warden. He walked the town making sure no one had lights on."

— Mary (Montgomery) Karch

1942: Dick Myers Jr. and friends David Hansen Jr. and Ulrik Hoff. Dick Myers Sr. owned the fishery and diner on the circle in Ship Bottom in addition to the Barnegat City pounds.

U.S. Lifesaving Station, Barnegat

Circa 1882: U.S. Lifesaving Station #17 would be expanded again around 1884. It had a keeper and crew in full uniform.

Haddock House and John W. Haddock

From the Memories of Morris Archer, Jr.

In October of 1897, John W. Haddock bought a house and property in Barnegat City, towards the end of East 4th Street, right along the ocean. He moved to Barnegat City with his wife Emeline Hunt, whom he had married in 1883.

"He had a lot of money, for that place at least. And he had a lot of money period for his

generation. He had a little powerboat, an internal combustion engine, it was just a small thing, just ran it around locally — channels, the inlet and bay. I think he had the first internal combustion engine in Barnegat City. I don't think anyone else had one. All the fishermen went in and out the inlet under sail, and of course across the bay under sail. I remember where he kept the thing. He had a little boathouse, where he would run it in for protection, connected directly with the water in the harbor where the Coast Guard is now. He used to fuss around there in his powerboat.

"He was a great guy for collecting the sculpture on the bow of the schooner [the figurehead] … I remember old Captain Lewis Sprague, who was quite a character around Barnegat Inlet, a retired schooner master of the Coast Guard schooner, he said that was a dangerous thing to do. He said the ocean never liked that, the ocean was going to get those things. He used to tell me that as a boy; I would stand looking at him, and he would say 'the ocean is going to get those" and I thought there was no way the ocean was going to come in there, quite a way away.

"The widow's walk was enclosed. They said that he added that… He had up there a wheel of a ship that he had acquired when he got some of this other lore from the sea. He was so mad that he would sit

Opposite: the eclectic backyard of the Haddock house. Left: the Haddock house is on the right. Notice how close it is to the water — this is its original site on 4th Street, around 1919.

up there in a hard northeaster and pretend he was putting a ship through the sea, heading it up in the wind..

"That place was quite nice. He had in the back there a little land. I remember he had a couple of peach trees, kind of like a miniature orchard, and he had an artesian well. The artisan well, curiously enough, as it flowed, came out of a big pipe in his back yard in the orchard. He couldn't use all the water and anybody who wanted to could come and get it and take a bottle water, because the town had no water.

"Of course the ocean came in and washed away the orchard and all of his stuff. Destroyed his place, but I guess that was after his death".

Dick Myers, owner of the Sunset, bought the Haddock house after a winter storm in 1920 washed out the Oceanic, flooded the garden of the Haddock house and washed away the relics of ships and statues. Once the water receded and the land dried, Dick Myers moved the house to Fifth Street, then a few months later moved the house yet again to its current position between 6th and 7th streets.

The Haddock house, on 4th Street.

The Town and Lighthouse Through Storms and Stress

1919, after a northeaster

The keeper's house after a northeaster, showing rip-rap placed there to provide protection from the encroaching sea.

Ted Barber — Memories of the jetty and keepers' house:

"Yeah, Luther Cox bought it from the government and he stripped it of copper and fittings and so forth and he paid the government I think $200 for it and he had a certain amount of time to get rid of it or else it would revert back to the government. The time ran on so he sold it to my father for $20. And my father got Sylanus Patterson, his horses and his man, and my brother and me, and we all tore it down. Gutted practically all, all but the bricks and got some of those, still got some of them. Beautiful bricks in that place. You can find bricks from the Oceanic up there on the beach. … What do they call them? rose-bricks. …All the ends are washed off, the ends are no longer square. They all look like a loaf of bread or cake.

"This shows you the erosion. You see… how the hills [dunes] washed away. And the high tide

Keeper's house, after a 1920 northeaster.

would come up and undercut the hills and they would fall down and then the ebb tide would come over and follow the course of the shore and carry the sand out to sea, out to the bar obviously and then the high tide again would pick the sand up, but it would deposit it on the other side on north beach (Island Beach) and north beach continued to grow while we continued to shrink".

"They built what you call a girdle or a skirt around the lighthouse. I think it was around '38 when they built that. But that's the beginning of the first rock jetty after the Sterling and Striker thing was washed away in about 1920. They decided to build another rock jetty to go out and parallel the inlet and that was built by Woolly and Howland, and I know because I worked for them, they were from Long Branch …And that groin worked fine except that eventually it kept sinking and was not effective."

Damage from winter storms (top) prompts the construction of a new jetty to protect the lighthouse in the summer of 1920. B.F. Archer is on the left.

Right: A clipping shows damage from the ice storm of February, 1920. The building in the center is the Haddock house; on the right is the Oceanic and the far left is the artisan well from the Haddock house.

Below: An unidentified man surveys the damage on the beach. The Haddock house has now been moved back from the beach, and half of the Oceanic has been demolished.

"They brought the rocks from the quarries. They ran through with a big tractor trailer, flat body, and dumped them down there. Had two big towers, and cabled them across the inlet .. . That was sometime in early '40s. We were fishing in and out of them."

— Holmes Russell

Circa 1943: This jetty construction project utilizes two towers, with cables to carry rocks across the inlet. The second tower was on Island Beach. The huge boulders were carried across the towers in leather buckets.

Joe Knight's bait shack at 7th Street, and some of the damage and debris from the '44 hurricane.

The Lighthouse

Barnegat Light, 1926, facing north. Photograph was taken from the upper porch of the Sunset Hotel. At this time the keeper's house is no longer there.

Memories of the Lighthouse:

"When they discontinued that as a maritime light, then they put a gas operated fixture on top of the lighthouse, I don't recall whether it turned on automatically or not, I think not, because they retained Mr. Applegate and then his son and that was their duty, to turn the light on and off and that was operated by gas. It was a steady light, it was not a revolving carriage with rays, illuminated by a kerosene candle."

— Ted Barber

"There were three houses. My brother at one time was there, I guess it was during the war period. He was pretty old to go to the war — that is the first World War. He was in the Navy. Anyhow, he had some kind of a job there at the lighthouse and what he did there he never told us. I didn't know anything about that, but I used to take his dinner up when I was home on vacation from college. I'd take his dinner after he'd gone up; early, because darkness came early — it was Christmas time — and walk up the steps... all the way up."

— Mrs. Zeber

The lens, now housed in the Barnegat Light Museum.

1927-29: Various views of the lighthouse. Photograph on right shows timbers used for jetty construction.

"Sparky" Dickerson out on a flounder fishing trip, passing by the bell buoy at the end of the south jetty, about 1948.

A Living from the Sea

Independent dock (Viking Village), West 18th Street, in 1930. The lighthouse may be the most familiar icon of this small fishing village, but this dock could well be the heart of the town. The dock began in 1927 with a dozen fishermen who put up enough money to get the project started.

"They wanted to have a place of their own and to be independent."

"They rented a truck and built that road, 18th Street They built that themselves by hand, they chopped down the trees and they built right to the dock. They asked if they could have the planking from the bridge... that first dock was built from the planking off the bridge.

"After a while they built their shacks, you know, to bait-up in... down there now they've got a bar and different things, but there were shacks for baiting-up when they cod-fished and also to keep their fisherman supplies."

— Mrs. David Hansen

In 1927 there were two rows of "bait-up" shacks, used for baiting codfish long-line gear. Clams were used for bait with the winter fish; each hook was on a leader line, attached an arms length apart on the long-line. In this photograph the fishermen are mending nets for summer fishing. Each fisherman was assigned his own shack. Today, only the shacks on the left remain, and have been converted to shops in "Viking Village".

"That Independent fishery started in 1927...we bought the land from Everett Jones, the whole block there, we started with $10 a piece. Big deal! We got the pilings for 25 cents each, hired a truck for $10 a day. The top deck from planks they tore up [from the old wooden bridge], we got for nothing. We borrowed every wheel barrow in town to make our own road. There was just meadows down there."

— Chris Halverson

Independent Dock.

Ingvald Dalland and Jens Jensen, with Reverend Kjeldahl, work on an engine.

Independent Dock. Tom Hansen and Ole Olsen untangling a net.

The original Independent Dock fishermen:

Sigurd Johnson
Ingvald Dalland
Edward Shoning
Otto Olsen
Siguard Salvensen
Peter Norstrand
Jens Jensen
John Larson
Axel Axelsen
Ole Larsen
Kristen Hauge
Axel Jacobsen
Engel Hoff
Dave Hansen
John Engelsen
Torgny Ingebretsen
Jack Svelling (Svellingsen)
Conrad Svelling (Svellingsen)
Chris Halversen
Lars Farland
Haakon Hansen
Louie Larsen
Evert Eliason
Pet Farland
Halfdon Hem
Martin Frank

John Engelsen and Jack Svelling wait for the running line to take the last pot (on rail of boat). There were 26 pots to a stringer, each with the potential to catch lobster, sea bass and mackerel.

Pot Fishing

"Pop (John Engelsen) worked with Mr. Myers for some time on the pounds, and then started with his own pot boat, fishing for himself. He was from Norway, came here in the early 1920s, seeking work and freedom"

— Ann (Engelsen) Surlick

1930, John Engelsen (left) and Axel Jacobsen standing in front of their lobster pots at the end of the season. The pots are set up to be cleaned and re-tarred, and will be stored in their bait-up shacks.

1930: During a lull, fishermen and local women pose in front of some pot boats at the Independent Dock. From left: Conrad Svelling, Torgny Ingebretsen, Jens Jensen, Doris Cobb, John Adolfsen, Edith Olsen, Axel Jacobsen. The boats were probably pulled ashore for scraping and painting.

"In the fall all of the traps had to be cleaned and re-tarred for the next season and we did all this by hand. The stringers, or line, had to all be replaced. Buoys were used for markers; we all knew our own set. We never had the equipment they have today. All we had was a compass — most of the time we didn't use that."

— Chris Halverson

Axel Jacobsen was a pot fisherman who came to Barnegat City in 1920, initially working on the pounds for Dick Myers. He later bought his own fishing boat, and fished well into the 1950s.

"There was no water there, we moved the first fish in by sneakboxes to get into the dock to ship. Then we started to tie the boat line alongside itself and then churned the channel with the propellers so we could run the boats in. It was just mud, no water in there, it was just mud all over there"

— Chris Halverson

John Engelsen, 1924, sitting by some net fishing boats at 18th Street dock. These skiffs were open; later they built cabins on them. Note the lack of water at low tide; by 1927 the area where the skiffs are on shore would be dredged out to make the basin larger.

David Hansen and his wife Evelyn tarring pots for the next season in front of Joahn Engelsen's boat house, 1930. Cleaning and re-tarring the pots had to be done each fall in preparation for the spring. Left: Hansen in 1934 with his catch.

"My man did cod fishing in the winter and pot fishing in the spring. It all was very hard work. Squidding season was a very important season for us; it brought in good money. We ate a lot of fish and potatoes. We all grew gardens."

— Mrs. David Hansen

Old Captain Sculthorp

A net fisherman since 1900, Captain Sculthorp, shown here in 1904, was one of the first people to net fish out of Barnegat City. He lived on 5th Street by the schoolhouse. His house was appropriately called the "Net Cottage".

Right: Len Wieczorek heading in, 1948. The building to the right of the lighthouse is "Andy's at the Light", a bait and tackle shop and restaurant owned by Andy Bjornberg. The store is still run by the family.

1948: Mary Ella, *a small sea bass charter boat owned by Mr. Copperthwait. To the right, beyond the boat, is Myers Pound fishery on West 6th Street.*

1924: Myers Pound house, along with other small boat houses in the area, was built from the remains of the Oceanic Hotel. The rest of the hotel wood was used for completing the pound's dock.

Circa 1925: Pound fishing boats at Myers Dock, West 6th Street. The catch was packed in wooden barrels. The boat with the cabin is a houseboat belonging to one of the fisherman, the large boat in the center is a Coast Guard boat; the rest are pound boats, all docked on the mud banks until the dock was built. The boat shed belongs to John Haddock.

Freda Benestad, John Engelsen and Morris Archer (right), age 12, at Myers Pounds in 1924. Engelsen often babysat for Freda when her mother Lola cooked for the men at the pound shed.

This pound house, circa 1924, is typical of those found up and down the island.

Below: Dickie Myers Sr., second from right, and some fisherman at his 6th Street dock. Right: Drying and repairing nets by the lighthouse.

"Dick Myers gave us a job on the pounds; my brother and I were very good at mending nets — this is the kind of work we did with our father in Norway. The pound pilings were 90 feet long —50 feet went into the ocean floor and the rest in the water, with enough sticking out so no boats would run them over. The nets were very heavy. All the nets were factory made; we just had to mend holes made by the bigger fish getting trapped in them. And of course storms tearing them up, or another boat running over them. We did this in the big field by the Sunset Hotel. The nets were often laid out to dry there too."

— Chris Halverson

Top: Ingvald Dalland, left, and Ingman Benestad (holding fish), dockmaster for Myers Pounds. Right: Netting fish out of the pound net.

Dick Myers' 6th Street pound. Fish pack-out has evolved from wooden barrels to wire baskets. Myers is wearing the white hat. Mrs. Myers (below, left) was the bookkeeper and was at the dock almost every day.

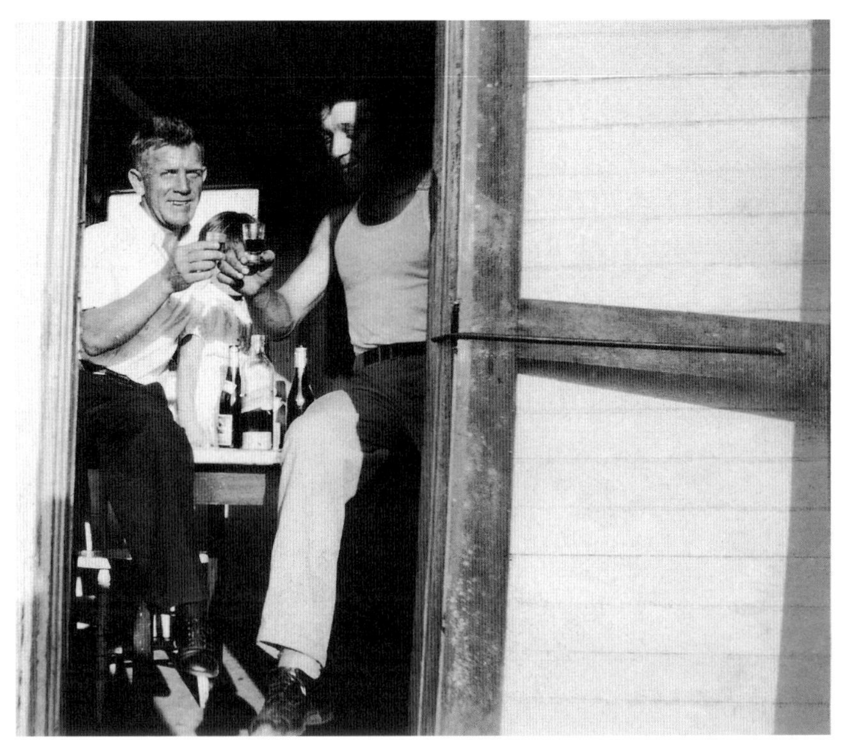

All the locals had a nickname — that was the way of the Scandinavians: “Dimpleman Charlie”, “Iron-Fat”, “Trix Bill Charlie”, “Cutie”, “Horse Charlie”, “Gentleman Charlie”, Fat Hands”, “The Yes Man”, “Double Axel”, “Lightship Ole”, “Big Ed”.

1930: John Engelsen and Axel Jacobsen propose a toast from John’s boat house by the bait-up shacks.

Below: Independent Dock, 1940s.

John Engelsen and three of the Sunset Girls, 1930.

Acknowledgments

1950: Theresa Montgomery, the author's sister, outside Inlet Deli.

This book would not have been possible without the help of friends and family who were wiling to share their time with me going over old photographs of Barnegat City. Freda Benestad Fackler, my high school English and gym teacher (her father was dockmaster on the pounds), shared the pound fishery pictures and the first Girl Scout Troop picture.

Gloria Hansen Braun, Doris Hansen, Sarah Hansen Millard, and Nora Hansen Bergman brought me four albums of pictures and newspaper clippings that their mother, Evelyn Hansen, made for them when she left Barnegat Light.

George Svelling, Barnegat Light fisherman, and his sister, Greta Svelling Purgavie of Ship Bottom, who took the time to go through their mother's old photo album.

Rolf Engelsen formerly of Barnegat Light, now resides in Florida, and his sister Ann Engelsen Surlick of Tuckerton. Their mother Frances Engelsen was a very busy woman who worked at the Sunset Hotel and still found time to take many pictures, which are scattered throughout the book, many of the Independent Dock and the Sunset Hotel.

Len Wicezorek and his wife Joan Montgomery of West Creek went through albums and found pictures of the bay and Lighthouse.

I thank Edith Dalland Parker and her sister Jane Dalland Aitken, for pictures of the Independent Dock and the Sunset Hotel with the landing dock.

Ron Spisso, a dear friend, made audio tapes of the old timers of Barnegat Light. From these, I received much information on the railroad, hotel life, and the beginning of the fishing industry. Ron was the owner of Inlet Deli, formerly Applegate's General Store and the post office.

Kirk Larson, mayor of Barnegat Light, let me read through the first minutes of the Borough of Barnegat City. This gave me my start for the time line, and a great story as to how the town began.

Others who gave information about their families are: Ann Bucher of Forked River; Richard Updyke (information on small steamers); William C. Brown (information on the Brown family); Jerry Walnut for information on his family, the Archers, and for all the time he spent with me at the Barnegat Light Museum; Mr. and Mrs. Robert Melchorie, two dear friends — many thanks to you both for all your support.

My thanks to all who helped in my travels into the past of Barnegat Light: Toms River Historical Society, Toms River; Barnegat Light Historical Society, Barnegat Light; Barnegat Historical Society, Barnegat. Many thanks to Margaret Thomas Buchholz for sharing Eleanor Smith's transcribed interviews with local fisherman of Barnegat Light; Dave Wood, Barnegat Light, for filling in a missing photograph; and Leslee Ganss for the great job designing this book. And for information and photographs on the lighthouse, keeper's house and Lifesaving Service, I credit the National Archives, Washington, DC.

Down The Shore Publishing offers other book and calendar titles (with a special emphasis on the mid-Atlantic coast). For a free catalog, or to be added to our mailing list, just send us a request:

Down The Shore Publishing
Box 3100
Harvey Cedars, NJ 08008

www.down-the-shore.com